YA BIO owens

12-2395

1713130

10/2011

DATE DUE

JUN 1 0 2016			
GAYLORD			PRINTED IN U.S.A.

D1516646

Jesse
OWENS

JESSE OWENS
Trailblazing Sprinter

By Chrös McDougall

Published by ABDO Publishing Company, 8000 West 78th Street, Edina, Minnesota 55439. Copyright © 2011 by Abdo Consulting Group, Inc. International copyrights reserved in all countries. No part of this book may be reproduced in any form without written permission from the publisher. SportsZone™ is a trademark and logo of ABDO Publishing Company.

Printed in the United States.

 THIS BOOK CONTAINS AT LEAST 10% RECYCLED MATERIALS.

Editor: Erika Wittekind
Copy Editor: Paula Lewis
Series Design: Christa Schneider
Cover Production: Christa Schneider
Interior Production: Sarah Carlson and Christa Schneider

Library of Congress Cataloging-in-Publication Data
McDougall, Chrös.
   Jesse Owens : trailblazing sprinter / by Chrös McDougall.
      p. cm. — (Legendary athletes)
   Includes bibliographical references and index.
   ISBN 978-1-61714-758-6
   1. Owens, Jesse, 1913-1980—Juvenile literature. 2. Track and field athletes—United States—Biography—Juvenile literature. 3. African American track and field athletes—Biography—Juvenile literature. I. Title.
   GV697.O9M33 2011
   796.42092—dc22
   [B]
                              2010046697

TABLE OF CONTENTS

CHAPTER 1

Jesse Owens practices in Berlin before the 1936 Olympics.

An Unlikely Friend

Jesse Owens, the American hope for three gold medals, was in trouble. On his second day of the 1936 Olympics in Berlin, Germany, Owens had tied his world record while winning the 100-meter dash. In the morning of the third day, he tied the Olympic record in the 200-meter dash preliminaries. Now facing the broad jump preliminaries, it appeared that he might not make the semifinals.

Owens was the clear favorite to win the event, which is now called the long jump. His personal best was more than a foot farther than that of his closest competitor, Luz Long of Germany. But before Owens could win a medal, he had to qualify for the finals. The first round of qualification was the quarterfinals. To move on to the afternoon's semifinals, Owens would need to jump 23 feet 5 1/2 inches (7.2 m). That should have been easy. Owens, now 22, had routinely jumped that far in high school. His personal best—also the world record—was 26 feet 8 1/4 inches (8.1 m). But after two jumps, he still had not passed it. Only one jump remained.

Owens's first attempt had been a mistake. No one had told him that practice runs were illegal that day, and he unknowingly ran down the runway and through the sandpit. That was common practice in the United States. But on this day, the officials called a foul.

Owens was shocked, but he maintained a calm presence on the outside. His nerves showed on the second jump. He hit the board squarely, but landed at only 23 feet 3 inches (7.1 m). Suddenly, the world record holder—the sure bet to win the Olympic gold medal— was in danger of being eliminated in the first round.

At this desperate moment, Owens received help from the most unlikely source, his closest competitor. Long said in his broken English:

> You know, you should be able to qualify with your eyes closed. Why do you not draw a line a few inches in back of the board and aim at making yourself take off from there? You'll be sure not to foul, and you certainly ought to jump far enough to qualify.[1]

Upon taking Long's advice, Owens easily qualified for the next round.

Racial Discrimination

It was unusual that an athlete would assist his main competitor. However, in 1936, it was even more unusual because of the two athletes' physical appearances. Long, who was tall and lean with blond hair and blue eyes, was considered to be the ideal Aryan. The Nazi Party, which ruled Germany, believed that all other races were inferior. The Nazis persecuted those other groups, especially the Jews.

To a somewhat lesser extent, the Nazis also discriminated against blacks, such as Owens. At the 1936 Olympics, the German newspapers referred to Owens and the 17 other blacks on Team USA as "auxiliaries," implying that they were not equal to their

Political Background

Among the reasons the United States decided not to boycott the 1936 Olympics was that the Olympics are traditionally supposed to be free of politics. However, when the visitors arrived in the summer of 1936, the political climate in Europe was heated. In 1935, the Nazis had declared that German Jews did not have as many rights as others. The Germans used technicalities to prevent all but one Jew from competing on the German Olympic team.

There was also tension over Germany's military rebuilding efforts. Germany had been disarmed following World War I. However, Adolf Hitler had been rapidly rebuilding the army. Just months before the Olympics, Hitler boldly led troops into the Rhineland, an area that Germany had lost in World War I and was now controlled by France.

Eventually, the Nazi persecution of Jews and other minorities led to the Holocaust. The Nazis systematically murdered 6 million Jews from 1933 to 1945. The aggressive Nazi military actions and invasion of Poland led to World War II.

Equipment

The shoes Owens wore when he was competing were made of kangaroo leather and had spikes on the bottom. The tracks were usually made of cinders, which were often uneven, and did not hold up well in rain. The athletes did not have starting blocks, so they dug holes to plant their feet at the starting line. Using modern track spikes, wind-resistant clothing, and a rubber track, Owens's performances would likely have been similar to those of elite athletes today.

white teammates.[2] Germany's ill treatment of Jews and others nearly caused some countries, including the United States, to boycott the Olympics. When visitors arrived, many were curious to see how the Germans reacted to the star US black athletes. By befriending Owens, Long defied the Nazis and their racist principles.

A Nazi Showcase

The Olympics had been awarded to Berlin in 1931 when Germany had a democratic government. However, two years later, Adolf Hitler and his Nazi Party took over that government and turned it into a one-party dictatorship. The Nazis began rebuilding the German army, which had been disarmed after World War I. The government also began regulating all aspects of German life, from industry to sport. It restricted basic human

Owens speaks to German competitor and friend Luz Long during the 1936 Olympics.

freedoms. The Nazis used propaganda to spread their message. Those who opposed Nazi views were persecuted.

Hitler wanted the 1936 Olympics to be the greatest ever and to showcase Nazi control over the country. To settle foreigners' fears about racial persecution and violence, the Nazis simply covered up signs of their racist policies during the Olympics. The government also ordered that anti-Semitic signs be taken down and that newspapers temporarily tone down their anti-Semitic language. Even the military presence was toned down with fewer uniformed soldiers visible throughout the city.

Many visitors had no idea of the terrible persecution taking place behind closed doors. Instead, they found an efficient, well-

> "In America, anyone can become somebody. Does that sound corny in this day and age? Well, it happened to me, and I believe it can happen to anybody in one way or another."[3]
> —*Jesse Owens*

run Germany. A record number of countries competed. The athletes marveled at the massive, world-class facilities. Although the racism had largely been hidden, the Nazi swastika was not. German pride filled the city—red and black Nazi flags hung from almost every building. Hitler ensured that he and the Nazi movement—not the athletes—were the center of attention.

Beyond the competitions, visitors were left impressed with the Nazis' thorough organization and control throughout the city. Many left with the impression of an open and happy Germany. And for the most part, the ceremonial aspects of the Olympics went as Hitler had planned. However, he could not control the results of the events.

A Welcome Reception

To the surprise of many, the German fans wildly embraced Owens and the other black athletes. And Owens, considered the greatest athlete in the world, did not disappoint. In the broad jump finals, he held off Long for the gold medal. Owens's distance of 26 feet 5 1/4 inches (8.1 m) set a new Olympic record. After Owens's final jump, he and Long embraced. They proceeded to parade around the track together, hand-in-hand, while Hitler sat in his suite approximately 50 feet (15.2 m) away. Owens said of Long:

Medal Count

The 18 black US athletes won 14 medals at the 1936 Olympics. Germany led all countries with 89 medals, 33 of which were gold. The United States was second with 56 medals, 24 of which were gold.

It took a lot of courage for him to befriend me in front of Hitler. You can melt down all the medals and cups I have, and they wouldn't be a plating on the 24-karat friendship I felt for Luz Long at that moment. Hitler must have gone crazy watching us embrace.[4]

Owens won four gold medals at the 1936 Olympics, setting one world record and setting or tying three Olympic records. Some credited Owens and the other black athletes at the 1936 Olympics with disproving Hitler's theory of Aryan supremacy. But despite his success and popularity in Berlin, Owens was still a second-class citizen back home.

Jesse Owens accepts his gold medal for the broad jump at the 1936 Olympics. Luz Long, *right*, of Germany won the silver medal.

CHAPTER 2

African-American field hands work in the fields in the late 1800s.

Son of a Sharecropper

Henry Cleveland Owens, Jesse Owens's father, was born and raised in Oakville, Alabama. His ancestors had been taken from Africa in the 1830s and brought to the United States as slaves. Henry's parents also had been slaves, before slavery was abolished in 1865. But Henry, born in 1878, could not be enslaved. Although slavery had been outlawed, blacks still did not have the same freedoms and opportunities as whites. This was especially true in southern states such as Alabama where slavery had been most common and racism was still widespread. Blacks could be fined and jailed for just about anything that upset whites. Even worse, they could be lynched.

Starting a Family

When Henry was 18, he married Mary Emma Fitzgerald. They lived in a small, rundown shanty, and Henry became a sharecropper, farming the land of former slave owners in return for a portion of the harvest. Soon, Henry and Emma started a family. By 1912, Emma had been pregnant 12 times, although three babies had died in childbirth. Still, they had three daughters—Ida, Josephine, and Lillie—and six sons—Prentice, Johnson, Henry, Ernest, Quincy, and Sylvester. Although they had decided nine children were enough, on September 12, 1913, Emma gave birth to James Cleveland Owens. They called him by his initials, J. C.

Sharecropping

Although the United States abolished slavery in 1865, blacks still did not have much opportunity to improve their lives. Following the war, many plantation owners could not afford to pay for farm labor, and freed slaves had no land to start their own farms. The development of sharecropping served the needs of both parties.

Many southern blacks, such as Henry Owens, became sharecroppers. Sharecroppers would live on former slave owners' property and work as farmers. In turn, the sharecropper would give part of the harvest to the landowner as rent.

This was a poor and insecure lifestyle. The former slaves had to purchase their own seeds and tools using credit, then pay the loan back after the harvest. Often these expenses, combined with the portion of the harvest that went toward rent, would come close to exceeding their income. This system kept the former slaves indebted to the landowners. While technically free, the debt meant that the former slaves had little control over their lives—essentially keeping them enslaved. Since many blacks, such as Henry, could not read or write, the landowners could easily take advantage of them.

J. C.'s family was poor, and he was often hungry. He suffered from illnesses such as chronic bronchial congestion and pneumonia. At various points in his childhood, his mother had to cut growths— likely fibrous tumors—off his body as well. The family could not afford to hire a doctor.

The Owens family walked nine miles (14.5 km) to Oakville Missionary Baptist Church, where Henry was a deacon, every Sunday. During the week, the black kids went to school in the same building. At the time, many public facilities were segregated, and the black-only facilities were usually of much lower quality. J. C.'s school did not have a paid teacher. The school shut down during the planting and harvesting seasons so students could help their families in the fields. J. C. barely learned to read and write.

A Mysterious Lump

When J. C. was five, he noticed a mysterious bump growing on his chest. Soon, it began to grow so large that it was pressing against his lungs and affecting his breathing. Emma had previously cut off a similar lump from J. C.'s leg, but she feared to do the same on his chest because it was so close to his heart. But the family could not afford a doctor, and she eventually removed it herself with a kitchen knife. The painful operation left a hole the size of a golf ball, and the incision continued to bleed for days. J. C. had likely suffered from a fibrous tumor.

Learning from Mom

J. C. inherited his mother's temperament. With a positive outlook on life, she was optimistic about her family's future and thought her kids could have a better life than she did. Henry was much less optimistic. He lived in fear of his white neighbors and was afraid to even look them in the eye.

J. C. did not know any other life, so he enjoyed his childhood, despite its hardships. "We used to have a lot of fun," he later told a friend. "We never had any problems. We always ate. The fact that we didn't have steak? Who had steak?"[1] Instead of shying away from whites as his father did, J. C. learned from a young age to smile a lot. If he was pleasant and polite, people would be more likely to think positively of him. During the summers, he joined his brothers and neighbors— black and white—at a local pond to swim and fish. He also enjoyed hunting opossums and sitting by a campfire. Not quite old enough to play baseball with his brothers, J. C. played other games, such as tag, with the other young kids.

What J. C. really liked, however, was to run. "He'd run and play like everybody else,"

"I always loved running. . . . I loved it because it was something you could do all by yourself, all under your own power. You could go in any direction, fast or slow as you wanted, fighting the wind if you felt like it, seeking out new sights just on the strength of your feet and the courage in your lungs."[2]

—*Jesse Owens*

his cousin said later, "but you never could catch him."[3] J. C. loved the freedom he felt when running; nobody could hold him back.

Moving North

Around the time J. C. was born, large numbers of Southern blacks were moving north. The new industrial and factory jobs in the North were viewed as better and more reliable than the farming jobs in the South. In some cases, machines replaced farm laborers. In addition, droughts or floods meant the sharecroppers made very little money at times. The Southern blacks saw opportunities for better jobs in the North. J. C.'s sister, Lillie, was among those moving north. Along with many others from northern Alabama, she moved to Cleveland, Ohio. Though racism still existed there, Cleveland offered

Northern Migration

During the early part of the twentieth century, an influx of industrial jobs in the northern United States opened up. This was partly due to World War I, when many men were at war and foreign immigration into the United States was limited. Many Southern blacks saw this as an opportunity to escape their poor and restricted lives in the South. More than 500,000 Southern blacks moved north between 1910 and 1920. From Alabama alone, more than 65,000 blacks moved north by 1920. Blacks were still discriminated against in the North, but not to the extent that they were in the South.

opportunities for blacks that were unmatched in places such as Oakville.

In Cleveland, Lillie found a well-paying job and a husband. She began writing to her family, encouraging them to join her in the North. One night, J. C. overheard his parents talking about moving. "We're nearly starving here," his mother said. "It's crazy to go on like this, Henry!"[4] In 1922, when J. C. was nine, the family moved to Cleveland—though Henry's hand shook in fear as he packed to leave.

A steel mill in Cleveland, Ohio

CHAPTER 3

Jesse Owens, *center*, with Fairmount Junior High School's champion outdoor track team, 1928

Moving to Ohio

The Owens family initially struggled with the transition from a rural town in the South to a major city in the North. They had settled in Cleveland's underprivileged East Side, and even Emma struggled with her new life. She was often afraid to go outside alone. Their neighborhood was known for crime, bootlegging, and prostitution. Racism and segregation still existed in Cleveland—and increased as blacks moved into the city and took the limited jobs. But the city was safer and provided more opportunities than Oakville. Groups such as the National Association for the Advancement of Colored People (NAACP) and the Urban League tried to help blacks find jobs in Cleveland. Henry and his three oldest sons found work at a steel mill. The money was better than what he earned as a sharecropper, but Henry was not happy there. He struggled to keep up with the younger, stronger workers.

Jesse Owens sits with his teammates at East Technical High School.

Jesse Owens

In Cleveland, J. C. enrolled at Bolton Elementary, which was three blocks from his home. As an integrated school, Bolton accepted children of all races. Still, J. C. was one of few blacks and was timid around his new classmates. On his first day, the teacher asked his name. He replied, but his quiet voice and Southern drawl were hard for the teacher to understand. "Jesse?" she asked for clarification. Too scared to correct her, he replied, "Yes, ma'am, Jesse Owens."[1] From that point forward, he was known as Jesse Owens.

Since he could barely read or write, the teachers at Bolton put Jesse in first grade, where he was two or three years older than his classmates. He was soon moved into the second grade. But throughout school, he was always older than his classmates.

After Bolton, Jesse moved to Fairmount Junior High, where he met Charles Riley. A short, middle-aged man with a thick Irish accent, Riley was the school's physical education teacher and track coach. Riley noticed Jesse's strong legs and how he outran and outjumped everybody in gym class.

When Jesse was 13, Riley approached him about running track. Jesse was so nervous that he could barely respond—in Alabama, white men rarely addressed blacks. But they soon agreed to start practicing together. Since Jesse had to work after school at a shoe repair shop, he agreed to train with Riley for 90 minutes each morning before school.

Jesse and Riley soon became like father and son.

Blacks in Track and Field

When Jesse was at the 1932 US regional track-and-field trials, he was surprised to see so many great black athletes. Whites had long dominated the sport, but blacks were beginning to emerge. At the 1932 Olympics in Los Angeles, four black men competed in track and field for Team USA: Eddie Tolan, Ralph Metcalfe, Edward Gordon, and Cornelius Johnson.

They spent the mornings working on Jesse's running form. Riley was a stickler for repetition. He made sure Jesse always ran in a relaxed manner with a straight head and high knees. On weekends, Riley would bring Jesse to join his family for lunch.

When Jesse was 15, Riley set up a 100-meter race along the sidewalk of East 107th Street in Cleveland. He was so shocked when Jesse finished in 11.0 seconds that he got a new stopwatch and timed Jesse again the next day, in case there had been a mistake. Jesse, again on a sidewalk and without track spikes, ran the distance in the same time. He was already among the fastest people in the world—of any age.

Jesse soon began setting records. In 1928, he set junior high world records in long jump and high jump. Jesse was very fast on the track, but he had a tendency

Booker T. Washington

Growing up, Jesse was intrigued by the life and works of Booker T. Washington. A famous black leader, Washington had died in 1915. He had preached to blacks that they patiently work for equality by improving their economic standing and race relations.

Washington also founded the Tuskegee Institute in Alabama.

There, students were taught vocational skills that Washington thought would help the poor Southern blacks more than a traditional college education.

"I know that the name of Booker T. Washington will live forever in the memory of the colored people," Jesse said later. "I would like to become a little bit like him."[2]

to fade before the race was over. Once he learned to relax and run hard for the entire race, Jesse was almost unbeatable.

Hard Times

In 1929, Henry Owens was hit by a car and broke his leg. He had struggled to keep a job in Cleveland, but now it was even harder for him to work. In 1929, the stock market crashed, and the country entered the Great Depression. Because Henry could no longer provide for his family, his kids began dropping out of school to find jobs.

By 1930, Jesse was the only sibling left in school. He enrolled at East Technical High School, where fewer than 5 percent of students were black. Like many blacks during the Depression, Jesse went to a vocational school. These schools taught trade skills instead of academics. In addition to track and field, Jesse made the football and basketball teams. He did not stick with either sport, deciding to focus his energies on track. Jesse was popular at East Tech. His classmates respected him as a star athlete and a leader, but he was also modest and friendly. The well-kempt boy was also a hit among the girls and soon had a steady girlfriend, Ruth Solomon.

Jesse and Riley were reunited at East Tech. The school's track coach had little experience, so he

Horse Sense

After a particularly frustrating race in which Jesse's face showed a lot of strain, Riley took him to the horse track. The eighth-grader and his coach watched the thoroughbreds all day. When the races were over, Jesse noted the relaxed stride and the calm faces of the horses. "The way they move . . . is like they're not trying. Like it's easy. But you know they are trying," he said.[3]

had asked Riley to help out. With Riley's assistance, Jesse continued to thrive.

Los Angeles, California, was selected as the site of the 1932 Summer Olympics. Although Jesse was only 18 years old, he had a chance to make the US team. That summer, he attended the US preliminary trials in Evanston, Illinois. It was the first time that he had raced against world-class opposition, and he struggled. Jesse did not qualify for the Olympic team that year, but watching the elite runners and jumpers at the trials motivated him to improve.

A Young Father

Shortly after Jesse competed at the US regional trials, he became a father. Ruth gave birth to Gloria Shirley Owens on August 8, 1932. Jesse was 18 and Ruth was only 16 at the time. Although they were not married yet, Jesse and Ruth planned to spend their lives together. For the time being, however, Ruth dropped out of school to take a job at a beauty parlor. Her family took responsibility for raising baby Gloria. Jesse, meanwhile, was still busy with track. Just days after Gloria was born, several European runners stopped in Cleveland on their way home from the Olympics. At a meet attended by more than 50,000 people, Jesse dominated his field in the 100-meter dash, winning in 9.6 seconds.

As a senior at East Tech, Jesse was named student council president and captain of the track team. He began to garner national attention as well. Fans were taken by his grace and the seriousness with which he approached the sport. Jesse's feet moved fast, but his moves looked effortless to the fans. Colleges from across the nation were interested in having him compete for them.

That summer, Jesse led his team to the National Interscholastic Championship in Chicago, Illinois. In addition to

Track Measurements

Measurements in track and field are traditionally done according to the metric system, which uses meters. However, in the early part of the twentieth century, running events in the United States were measured using the imperial system, which uses feet and yards. One yard is three feet—approximately .91 meters. While international competitions such as the Olympics used the 100-, 200-, and 400-meter dashes, for example, some meets in the United States used the 100-, 220-, and 440-yard dashes. Most US track meets now use metric measurements.

winning the broad jump, Jesse set a new world record in the 220-yard dash, as well as tied the world record in the 100-yard dash. He accounted for more than half of his team's points that day and finished his high school career having won 75 of the 79 races he entered. Upon returning home to Cleveland, Jesse was the focus of a victory parade through the city. But he would not stay long. He would soon leave Cleveland for Columbus, Ohio.

Jesse Owens as a student at East Technical High School in Cleveland, Ohio, in 1933

Jesse Owens leaps a hurdle during a collegiate competition in Berkeley, California, on June 22, 1935.

The Buckeye Bullet

When Owens became a high school senior, people around the country began to take notice of his college choices. At the time, approximately 15 percent of Americans went to college. A much smaller percentage were black. For Owens, who struggled in school and did not have much money, going to college would not have been an option had it not been for track and field. Some people in the black community had strong opinions about where he should go. They felt that Owens should attend— and thus bring attention to—a school that had a history of welcoming blacks. However, no historically black colleges reached out to Owens, and he never considered going to one. His track-and-field prospects were much better at a more mainstream college.

Owens selected Ohio State University. Many blacks were upset that Owens selected Ohio State. The school, along with the city of Columbus, Ohio, had a reputation for poor race relations.

Opposition

One black newspaper, the *Chicago Defender*, was particularly critical of Owens's decision to go to Ohio State. The newspaper wrote that a decision to attend Ohio State meant that Owens sanctioned "hate, prejudice, and proscription" because the school still segregated black and white students.[1]

"He will be an asset to any school, so why help advertise an institution that majors in prejudice?" wrote one editor.[2]

But the school was a track-and-field power and offered Owens good employment. Today, schools can offer scholarships to help athletes pay for schooling. But in the 1930s, scholarships were uncommon and sometimes illegal. Instead, schools would set athletes up with a job. Owens worked as an elevator operator at the state capitol building in Columbus.

As some had predicted, life in Columbus was not welcoming. Owens was barred from living with whites in the dorms, and most restaurants refused to serve him. At his job, Owens was assigned to the service elevator unseen by the public. He struggled in the classroom and was on academic probation after two terms. But as usual, Owens tried to make the best of his situation. After all, he was there for athletics. At the beginning of his second term, he had been named to the 1933 All-America Track and Field Team by the Amateur Athletic Union (AAU).

A New Coach

Owens first met his new coach, Larry Snyder, during his freshman year. Snyder was only in his second year as head coach when Owens arrived. But he was already well known. An Ohio State track star in the 1920s, Snyder nearly made the 1924 Olympic team before being injured. As a coach, he was young—only about ten years older than Owens—and a bit quirky. For example, Snyder had the unorthodox habit of having his athletes train to music. Owens and Snyder immediately respected each other. The young coach was

Views on Black Athletes

As Owens and other black athletes were breaking out as stars in track and field, there were many misconceptions as to why the blacks were so fast. One theory was that blacks had more speed because they were more primitive. "It was not so long ago that his ability to sprint and jump was a life-and-death matter to him in the jungle," said Dean Cromwell, the coach at the University of Southern California.[3] Another theory, which was supported by Snyder, was that blacks had a different cell structure in their nervous systems. He believed that blacks were able to release strong jolts of energy, which allowed them to be faster and more powerful.

Another popular theory was that blacks had different bone and muscle structure than whites. A doctor in Cleveland examined Owens in search of physical attributes that might be unique to blacks. The doctor x-rayed Owens's leg bones, examined his muscles and joints, and took measurements of his limbs. However, he discovered nothing unusual based on Owens's race—only that Owens was in great shape.

also impressed with Owens's athleticism, specifically his quick feet.

Freshmen were allowed to train, but they could not compete in college athletics. To create a buzz around his freshman star, Snyder set up exhibitions to showcase Owens's talent. By the end of the season, Owens had broken the school record in the long jump and had outrun other records. Track and field was popular, although not as much as baseball and boxing. But when Jesse Owens competed, the crowds increased.

After the school year and some AAU meets, Owens returned home to Cleveland. He had claimed that he and Ruth were to be married that summer, but they did not. He headed back to Columbus in the fall and began his first varsity indoor season that winter. When the team traveled, the blacks were usually barred from the hotels and restaurants that accepted their white teammates. Owens was also at a disadvantage because Ohio State did not have indoor training facilities. But he still won most of the races he entered, and his popularity grew.

More Records

Although Owens is popularly credited with breaking three world records and tying another at the 1935 Big Ten Conference Championships, he was actually recognized for breaking two more. The 200-meter dash and 200-meter hurdles are slightly shorter than the 220-yard events that Owens ran. Timers at the 200-meter marks recorded Owens as the fastest person to ever run the two metric events as well.

The Meet of His Life

Five days before the 1935 Big Ten Conference Championships, Owens hurt his back. He had been roughhousing with his Alpha Phi Alpha fraternity brothers when he fell down a flight of stairs. Now, sitting at Ferry Field in Ann Arbor, Michigan, with 12,000 fans waiting to see him, Owens did not know if he could compete.

The fans were eager to see "the Ebony Antelope."[4] In his previous meet, he had set the world record in the 220-yard dash and had tied the record in the 100-yard race. But now he could barely move. Even a long bath the night before and constant massages did little to unlock the pain. Snyder tried to convince Owens not to run. At one point, he said he was going to pull Owens from the meet. But that was enough to get Owens on his feet and to the track for his first event. Without warming up, Owens ground his feet into the cinder track and set himself for the 100-yard dash. When the gun sounded, adrenaline took over, and his pain was gone. Six stopwatches timed him, and the

Still Dominant

Owens's broad jump at the 1935 Big Ten Conference Championships still stands as one of the best performances ever. His distance of 26 feet 8 1/4 inches (8.13 m)—without the benefit of new technology and training methods—would have been good enough for seventh place at the 2008 Olympics in Beijing, China. His world record stood for 25 years before it was finally surpassed. American athlete Ralph Boston surpassed him in 1960 with a jump of 26 feet 11 1/4 inches (8.21 m).

rules of the day dictated that the slowest time clocked was a runner's official time. Owens's official time was 9.4 seconds, tying the world record, but more than half the officials had clocked him at 9.3.

Fifteen minutes later, Owens was at the broad jump. He ran down the runway and, with perfect form, set a new world record—26 feet 8 1/4 inches (8.1 m). It was more than half a foot farther than the prior record. Ten minutes later, Owens was back on the track for the 220-yard dash. Again, without a hint of pain, he set a world record with 20.3 seconds. It was the first time anyone had set two world records in one day. But Owens was not done yet.

His final event, and his weakest, was the 220-yard hurdles. Owens did not like the hurdles, and his form was poor. But with the team title on the line, he agreed to race. The pain briefly came back, but it was gone as he ran toward the first hurdle. As usual, his form going over the hurdles was terrible. But his speed in between them was unmatched. Owens crossed the finish line in 22.6 seconds, beating the old world record by 0.4 seconds.

The crowd, which included Owens's old mentor Riley, went wild. They had just witnessed one of the greatest performances in the history of track and field.

Jesse Owens as an Ohio State University athlete, pictured with coach Larry Snyder

Jesse Owens wins the broad jump event at the NCAA championships in Chicago on June 20, 1936.

A Series of Setbacks

After his performance at the 1935 Big Ten Conference Championships, Owens was a bona fide superstar. Only 21 years old, he was among the top athletes in the world. Wherever he went, fans clamored to see and touch him. Along with his new fame, however, came pressure. The press scrutinized his every move. As a famous, successful black man, he also became a representative of the black community. His actions could affect how people viewed blacks in the United States. After the Big Ten meet, Owens headed to California for a series of competitions. He did not break any records in his three meets there, but he did win all eight events he entered. His personal life also became major news for the first time.

While in California, Owens met an affluent black woman named Quincella Nickerson. She invited Owens to her house for dinner, and their flirtation was well documented by the press. "So important is this man, that his love affairs

Amateur Athletic Union

The Amateur Athletic Union (AAU) was formed in 1888 to govern and standardize amateur athletics in the United States. When Owens was competing, the AAU represented US athletes in international competition. Although there was an American Olympic Committee, the AAU provided funding for US athletes and organized the various Olympic Trials. The Amateur Sports Act of 1978 changed that. The bill appointed the newly named US Olympic Committee to oversee amateur sports and their national governing bodies. The AAU then switched its focus to running amateur sports programs around the country.

have become front page news in the daily papers," reported the *Cleveland Call and Post*.[1] Naturally, Ruth Solomon was not happy. The mother of Owens's three-year-old daughter was home in Cleveland and still expecting Owens to marry her.

Ruth threatened to sue Owens for breach of promise. The news affected Owens, and he struggled at the AAU National Championships in Nebraska. People in the press began questioning whether Owens was still the fastest man in the world. Some felt his rivals, Eulace Peacock and Ralph Metcalfe, were faster. After the AAU meet, Owens rushed home to Ruth, and they married on July 5, 1935. Owens did not stay long, however. The next day he was back on the road for more track meets.

Owens redeemed himself by his successes on the track that summer. He was also named the first black captain of the Ohio State track team. But off-track issues continued to follow him. Earlier in 1935,

Ruth Solomon and Jesse Owens, date unknown

Owens had left his job as an elevator operator to become a page in the Ohio Statehouse. His new job paid better and was more respectable. But soon, he was under scrutiny from the AAU. Amateur athletes could be paid only for legitimate work, and the AAU was concerned that Owens was paid for work he did not do. That controversy, as well as Owens's struggles in the classroom, made for a tense time. The AAU decided in favor of him on August 31. However, it was not long before Owens faced another controversy.

Potential for an Olympic Boycott

In 1933, Adolf Hitler and the Nazi Party took control of the German government. Hitler quickly began establishing himself as a dictator, taking control of all aspects of life in Germany.

As the 1936 Olympics in Berlin approached, calls for boycotts became more frequent. In 1933, the AAU had said it would not support the Olympic Games in Germany if Jews were barred from the event. In turn, the Germans made empty promises that Jews would not be banned.

The American Olympic Committee—hesitant about mixing sports with politics—visited Germany in 1934 and declared that the discrimination was not as bad as the horror stories that had been reported. In actuality, the

Snubbed

Owens struggled with the controversy over whether he was illegally receiving money as a page in the Ohio Statehouse. His confidence took another blow in December 1935. Due to the job controversy, the AAU did not include Owens as one of ten finalists for the Sullivan Memorial Award. The award honors the nation's best amateur athlete.

Germans had covered up the discrimination when the committee and others visited.

The black community had mixed views on a boycott. Blacks—like all other non-Aryans—would be discriminated against in Germany. However, some argued that the treatment of German Jews was no worse than the treatment of blacks in the United States. They argued that it was hypocritical to boycott when much of the United States—including the major league sports leagues—were segregated.

It was difficult for Owens, now 22 years old, to decide what to do. The stories he heard about Germany sounded similar to his life in Alabama. But he faced pressure from some black organizations and newspapers, especially in Cleveland, to support the boycott. After working so hard at track and field, the Olympics could be the pinnacle of Owens's athletic career. Now people were telling him to sacrifice that.

Owens initially said he would not go to the Olympics if the Germans continued to discriminate against Jews. After that, Snyder spoke with Owens and convinced him to change his mind. "Why should we oppose

A Diverse Team

Some people argued that the US treatment of blacks in 1936 was as bad as the German treatment of Jews. Others pointed to the 100-meter dash finals at the US Olympic Trials as evidence to the contrary. In Germany, Jews had essentially been banned from the Olympics. In the United States, four of the seven finalists were black—and two of the seven were Jewish.

Germany for doing something that we do right here at home?" Snyder asked reporters, pointing out that Owens and other blacks had recently not been invited to a meet in New Orleans, Louisiana.[2] Some Jewish-American athletes, such as Marty Glickman and Sam Stoller, disapproved of the boycott for the same reason.

Despite the pressure, Owens and other star black athletes, including Ralph Metcalfe, Eulace Peacock, Ben Johnson, and Cornelius Johnson, signed a letter to American Olympic Committee President Avery Brundage saying they wanted to go. On December 8,

The Other 1936 Olympics

Before 1992, the Summer and Winter Olympics occurred during the same calendar year. In February 1936—approximately six months before the Summer Olympics kicked off in Berlin— Germany also hosted the Winter Olympics. The Games took place in Garmisch-Partenkirchen, two small towns on the edge of the Bavarian Alps.

The Winter Olympics were conducted on a smaller scale than the Summer Olympics. But the Garmisch-Partenkirchen Games were a sign of things to come in Berlin that summer. The Nazis spent $1.2 million building facilities for the Olympics, including a stadium that fit 50,000 people for the Opening Ceremonies. In trying to portray an open country, anti-Semitic signage was removed, and a Jew named Rudi Ball was made the star of the German hockey team. "Not the slightest evidence of religious, political or racial prejudice is outwardly visible here," a New York Times reporter wrote.[3] However, a strong military presence remained. Hitler and many of his top officials were visible throughout the Games.

1935, after a heated debate, the AAU narrowly voted against the boycott. An AAU boycott would not have prevented the American Olympic Committee from sending a team to the Olympics, but it would have caused many logistical problems.

One Last Step

Although Owens had committed to attending the Olympics, he still had to qualify. That winter, he faced another setback when he failed a psychology class. He was still allowed to practice with Snyder, but he was banned from competing. As team captain, Owens was naturally upset. But as Snyder pointed out, the situation had a bright side. Owens had competed so much during the prior summer that he had become worn out. Owens was humbled by the decision

Snyder's Support

Some people criticized Larry Snyder for convincing Owens not to boycott the Olympics. But Snyder—who was against Nazi policies—saw the 1936 Olympics as Owens's only opportunity to compete at that level. "Jesse Owens is sitting on top of the world today," he said. "If he continues to participate in this activity [the boycott], he will be a forgotten man."[4] As it turned out, the 1940 and 1944 Olympics were both cancelled due to World War II. Had Owens not competed in 1936, it is unlikely that he would have ever competed in the Olympic Games.

and vowed to work hard to improve. He soon did just that. That spring, his grades had improved, and he was eligible to compete again. He came back strong and quickly renewed his rivalry with his friend Peacock. As Owens continued to improve, however, Peacock suffered an injury and never fully returned to form.

In July, Owens arrived at Randall's Island in New York City for the US Olympic Trials. As most expected, he won the 100- and 200-meter dashes as well as the broad jump, qualifying for the Olympics in all three events. He was one of 18 black athletes who would be representing Team USA in Germany. Several days after the US Olympic Trials, Owens and Team USA boarded the SS *Manhattan* to cross the Atlantic Ocean. Next stop: Berlin.

Jesse Owens and Ruth Solomon take their marriage vows
on July 5, 1935.

Jesse Owens makes a practice attempt at the broad jump aboard the SS *Manhattan* while en route to the 1936 Olympics.

The 1936 Olympics

After nine days on the SS *Manhattan*, the 382 US athletes arrived in Germany. Owens tried to stay in shape while on the ship and was confident when he arrived in Berlin. Despite the concerns, both racial and political, the US delegation was greeted warmly by the Germans. The Berlin mayor and a waltz band ceremoniously welcomed Team USA to the city. The team found Berlin to be clean and organized while seemingly free of Nazi hatred. Owens was pleased to find that the athletes' village had many amenities and featured a wide array of food choices.

The American blacks, especially Owens, were of particular interest to the Germans. Photographers and autograph seekers mobbed Owens wherever he went. Memorabilia seekers stole two of his three pairs of shoes. With much less security than modern Olympic events, fans were able to crowd Owens while he was training. They even stood outside his window in the athletes' village, clicking pictures and requesting autographs. Despite the distractions, Owens was characteristically positive during the eight days before the Olympics. Life was good for the greatest athlete in the world.

Let the Games Begin

The 1936 Olympics began on August 1 with the opening ceremonies. In typical Nazi fashion, the ceremony was filled with pageantry. An air of excitement flowed in and around Olympic Stadium. Fans had lined up outside the stadium hours before the start, hoping just to catch a glimpse of Hitler on his way in. Inside, 110,000 excited fans packed the stadium. When Hitler arrived, the crowd was in a frenzy, and most saluted the leader. He had succeeded in putting the spotlight on himself and the Nazis.

When the athletes began to march in, the fans watched closely to see which countries saluted Hitler as they walked by. The crowd cheered for those that did salute. Two countries that did not salute were the United States and Great Britain. Traditionally, the US team does

Olympic Broadcast

Owens did not attend the opening ceremonies, but he was still able to see some of the event. The Germans set up a closed-circuit feed to provide some of the first-ever television sports broadcasts. The image was very crude, however, and it was difficult to make out the picture on the small screens available at the time.

not take part in that gesture, and in 1936, the team was the only nation that did not dip its flag when passing Hitler. The ceremonies had succeeded in showcasing German patriotism and Nazi grandeur. One reporter described the event as a "demonstration of Nazi organizing efficiency, a personal tribute to Adolf Hitler and pageant such as the modern world seldom has witnessed."[1]

Owens, however, did not march with Team USA. He remained at the athletes' village, relaxing for his first race the next day.

Helene Mayer

By taking advantage of technicalities, the Nazis essentially banned Jews from representing Germany at the 1936 Olympics. However, they made one exception. Helene Mayer, a half-Jewish woman who was studying in California, represented Germany in fencing. The Nazis ordered the German press not to report her Jewish ancestry. After winning a silver medal, Mayer—like all German medalists—gave the Nazi salute from the podium.

Gold Medalist

Owens's first test might have been his biggest. The first day of the Olympics featured one of the most popular events: the 100-meter dash. The day was cold and rainy when Owens woke up, conditions that were not ideal for a cinder track. But the confidence Owens had been feeling carried into his first day of competition. While others were tense, Owens was his usual relaxed and calm self on the 45-minute bus ride to the stadium.

The first round of preliminaries was comprised of 12 heats. The best athletes then qualified for the afternoon's quarterfinals, and the next day's semifinals and finals. Owens was the clear favorite for the entire event, so preliminaries were not of much concern. However, the proud German crowd, saluting Hitler throughout the day, was enthusiastic. "I had braced him for a stony, forbidding silence, because I had read all about the Germanic worship of the Aryan-supremacy

Hitler's Behavior

Many people were anxious to see how Hitler would respond to the black US athletes. After the first day of competition, Hitler publicly congratulated two German medalists and one Finnish medalist in his suite. But that afternoon, when the black US high jumpers Cornelius Johnson and Dave Albritton won gold and silver, Hitler was gone. A subheading in the *New York Times* the next morning read: "Hitler ignores Negro medalists."[2]

After day one, the president of the International Olympic Committee told Hitler that he either had to congratulate every athlete or none. Hitler chose none. Owens won his first medal on day two. Afterward, he claimed that he saw Hitler smile and wave at him. But the US press, unaware that Hitler was told not to publicly greet the athletes, was more sensational. "Hitler Snubs Jesse" was the headline on the *Cleveland Call and Post*.[3]

It is uncertain whether Hitler purposely left before greeting the black athletes on day one. It is also uncertain whether he actually waved at Owens. But later in life, Owens began repeating the story that Hitler had snubbed him.

idea," Snyder said.[4] But the reaction was just the opposite. To Hitler's dismay, the crowd rose to cheer the black star they had heard so much about. Owens, living up to expectations, won his first race in 10.3 seconds, tying his world record. That afternoon, he ran even faster while winning his quarterfinal heat. He did not beat the world record, however, because of a strong wind. Nonetheless, the fans were mesmerized by the grace and ease with which Owens ran.

When he returned to the Olympic Stadium the next day, he won his semifinal heat in 10.4 seconds. That evening, fresh and confident as ever, Owens took his position for the finals. He held off his rival Ralph Metcalfe for the gold medal. He again tied his world record time of 10.3 seconds. Basking in the cheer from more than 100,000 fans, Owens said, "This is the happiest day in my life. I guess it's the happiest I will ever have."[5]

Continuing On

The competition continued the next day. In between rounds of the broad jump competition, Owens set and then tied the world record for the 200-meter dash around a curve. His time was 21.1 seconds. After Luz Long helped Owens avoid disaster in the broad jump preliminaries that afternoon, Owens went on to win the broad jump. Even after securing the gold

Owens and Long

After competing in the broad jump, Owens and Luz Long met at the athletes' village. The two athletes spent the next several hours engaged in a heart-to-heart discussion even though Long struggled with his English. Owens and Long had vastly different backgrounds, but they became close friends at the 1936 Olympics. When Owens left the country, they promised to keep in touch. They often wrote to each other in the following years. But in 1943, Long, who had joined the German army, was killed in World War II.

medal, Owens still took his final jump. His leap of 26 feet 5 1/4 inches (8.06 m) set a new Olympic record.

Following the early success of Owens and the other black athletes, the German press became more hostile. Some German newspapers suggested that the American team could only win by sending black athletes instead of what they believed to be true Americans. Meanwhile, some US newspapers accused Hitler of snubbing Owens and other black athletes by not shaking their hands. Owens was again able to distance himself from the racial issues of the games. In typical positive fashion, Owens claimed that Hitler had waved at him after the broad jump medal ceremony.

On the fourth day, the crowd was still behind Owens. The superstar of the Olympics easily qualified for the 200-meter finals. Then, with no serious competition, he dominated the finals with a run of 20.7 seconds. He set the new world record for a curved track. And his Olympic experience was over—or so he thought.

The American 4 x 100 relay team, *from left*: Jesse Owens, Ralph Metcalfe, Foy Draper, and Frank Wykoff

The Relay

Owens had offered to run in the 4 x 100 relay. But the coaches said he would not be needed. They wanted to give some other athletes a chance for glory. However, on Day 6, the coaches abruptly changed their minds. They claimed that rumors had circulated about a very strong German team. The final decision was to have Owens lead off, followed by Ralph Metcalfe,

Foy Draper, and Frank Wykoff. Marty Glickman and Sam Stoller would go home without competing in the Olympics. This immediately caused controversy. Some believed favoritism played a part in the decision. One of the US coaches was Dean Cromwell, who also coached at the University of Southern California (USC). Both Wykoff and Draper competed for USC. Others accused the US coaches of anti-Semitism in an effort to avoid further embarrassing Hitler. Glickman and Stoller were the only Jewish members of the team.

Nonetheless, the US team dominated. In the preliminaries, Team USA tied the world record at 40.0 seconds. That afternoon, the US team beat second-place Germany by 15 yards. They also set a world record of 39.8 seconds. With four gold medals, Owens was the star of the Olympics. After so much competition and constant requests for pictures or autographs, he was also worn out. But he was given no time to rest after his dominating performance.

Jesse Owens and teammate Frank Wykoff work out in the Olympic village.

CHAPTER 7

Jesse Owens waves to the crowd during a parade in New York City after returning from the 1936 Olympics.

No Longer an Amateur

After the 1936 Olympics, Jesse Owens was a global star. Yet he was still bound by the restrictions of the Amateur Athletic Union. On the evening that he had helped win the 4 x 100 relay in Berlin, Owens was told to pack his bags. Because the AAU and American Olympic Committee had not raised enough money before the Olympics, they organized exhibition meets throughout Europe to make up the difference. Owens and other US athletes were the star attractions. Since they were amateurs, they could not make any money from the meets. But, the AAU would take home a portion of the gate receipts from the meets.

Snyder was incensed when he learned this. He felt the AAU had not fully explained to the athletes what these exhibitions entailed. The athletes had agreed to do the events before the Olympics, before they were worn out. In the past seven days, Owens had run ten races and competed in the broad jump. Now he was tired and homesick.

But with no other options, he packed his bags and joined his teammates on the exhibition circuit.

Exhibitions in Europe

The first stop was Cologne, Germany. Track and field was very popular in Europe, and 35,000 fans showed up to see Owens in Cologne. Exhausted, Owens struggled in his broad jump and relay events. In the featured event, the well-rested Ralph Metcalfe easily defeated Owens in the 100-meter dash. The meet had started at 6:00 p.m. and lasted a little more than two hours. Afterward, a banquet kept the athletes out

Mixed Opinions

When Owens announced that he was going to turn professional, people had differing opinions. Those closest to Owens were generally supportive. "It would be foolish for me to stand in Jesse's way," Snyder said. "He's absolutely at the height of his fame now."[1] Eulace Peacock, one of Owens's biggest rivals before the Olympics, said, "After the glory is gone, what have you? Jesse made a smart move."[2]

Others were more cautious. They wondered if the offers would actually result in any money or if they were scams. "Are all of these offers real?" an editorial in the *Cleveland Call and Post* asked. "Unfortunately a gang of people like to rush into print with fabulous sums mentioned for the services of reigning popular heroes, without any intention of making good, simply imbued with the idea of gaining free publicity."[3] Others wondered if his decision was shortsighted. They questioned how it would affect his eligibility at Ohio State where he had yet to earn a degree.

until around midnight. Then, the next morning, they had to be awake early to catch the plane to Prague, Czechoslovakia.

Owens was still the star attraction. But life was not glamorous for the man who had just won four gold medals for his country. With no local money that could be used in Prague, Owens only had lunch when someone bought him a sandwich and glass of milk on the plane. After landing in Prague at 4:30 p.m., the athletes had only 90 minutes to prepare for the track meet.

With no money and little time, they barely saw one city before moving on to the next. After Prague, the athletes went to Bochum, Germany, and then on to London, England. They did not know what their next stop would be until an official handed them their tickets before boarding a train or flight.

By the time they arrived in London, the athletes were tired, and some were getting sick. Again, they had little food, and the accommodations were bare. On the first night, they slept on cots at an old airplane hangar. Owens tried to stay positive and did his best to fulfill the constant requests for

"This track business is becoming one of the great rackets in the world. It doesn't mean a darn thing to us athletes. The AAU gets the money. It gets all the money collected in the United States and then comes over to Europe and takes half the proceeds. A fellow desires something for himself."[4]
—*Jesse Owens*

pictures and autographs. After London, the athletes were scheduled to compete in Sweden and elsewhere in Scandinavia. But this time, Owens and Snyder had second thoughts.

Turning Pro

As Owens was one of the country's most famous men at the time, he began receiving job offers in the United States. Many were show business offers. A California orchestra offered Owens $25,000 to tell jokes on stage for two weeks. Other more lucrative offers began coming in, too. Homesick and tired, Owens began to consider these offers. "I'm anxious to finish my college course," he said, "but I can't afford to miss this chance if it really means big money. I can always go back and get a degree."[5] Snyder made it clear that he would support whatever decision Owens made.

In London, Owens ran his last race as an amateur athlete. Running the third leg of a 4 x 100 yard relay, Owens set another world record. But after the meet, he decided he was finished. He would not travel to Scandinavia. The next morning, Avery Brundage, the president of the AOC, indefinitely suspended Owens from AAU-sponsored competition. A few days later, on August 19, Owens and Snyder boarded the *Queen Mary* to sail to New York.

Welcome Home

No matter how famous Owens had become at the Olympics, he would still be judged by the color of his skin at home. His parents, wife, and brother traveled to New York City to meet him. However, they were continuously denied a hotel room because they were black. Only after a white Cleveland councilman intervened were they able to secure lodging.

The reception became more positive after that. Reporters mobbed Owens as he disembarked from the *Queen Mary* on August 24. That was also the first time he had seen Ruth in two months. After answering some press questions, he set off for meetings. The world-famous athlete had a busy schedule. While in Europe and on the trip home, various businesspeople had made offers to Owens. One of them was Bill "Bojangles" Robinson, a famous tap dancer and entertainer. In New York City, Owens and his family visited Bojangles's house.

A Fiery Conversation

When Owens decided he was going home, the AAU wanted an explanation. Dan Ferris, the secretary-treasurer of the AAU, called Snyder from Berlin. After confirming the story, Ferris told Snyder that he was suspending Owens.

Before slamming the phone down, Snyder replied, "You can't suspend him from the Big Ten, because that's one organization you don't run. And listen, you're spending money on this call that could be spent on making up Olympic deficits."[6]

A Merry Journey

Owens's trip home from Europe was much more enjoyable than his trip to Europe. Without having to worry about an upcoming competition, Owens was able to eat as much as he wanted and to stay up late dancing. While traveling in Europe, Owens had lost 10 pounds (4.5 kg). On the trip home, he gained more than that back. The return trip was considerably shorter, too. The *Queen Mary* sailed from England to New York in a record four days, seven hours.

Owens did not stay in New York very long. The track star was greeted as a hero in his adopted home state of Ohio. In Cleveland, a victory parade awaited. At the end, 4,000 people were there for a ceremony at City Hall. Then he went to Columbus, Ohio, and did it all again. Throughout it all, Owens received gifts and praise and promises of money before heading back to New York City. Owens was no longer an amateur.

With visions of commercial deals coming his way, Owens joined the rest of the Olympic team three weeks after the Olympics ended for a parade through New York City. For the most part, the response was positive. But in Harlem, a mostly black neighborhood, people were still wary of segregation. Owens was at the front of the procession, next to a white boxer who refused to fight blacks. The other black stars from the Olympics were at the end. But at that time, nothing could bring Owens down. "For a time at least, I was the most famous person in the entire world," he said.[7]

Jesse Owens and his wife, Ruth, are greeted by fans when they return to Ohio following the 1936 Olympics.

CHAPTER 8

Jesse Owens prepares to race a horse on December 26, 1936.

Money Maker

Owens had rushed home from Europe to cash in on lucrative business offers. He soon discovered that most of them were bogus. Some had merely been publicity stunts—a way for a businessman to see his name in the newspaper. There was still a chance that some of the offers would eventually pan out, such as his plan to work with Bojangles. But in the meantime, no one had paid a cent to "the season's most publicized black man," as *Time* magazine reported.[1] Humbled by the situation, Owens knew he now needed to earn money in some way.

He found that payday in politics. In 1936, Alf Landon challenged incumbent Franklin D. Roosevelt for the presidency of the United States. Both the Republicans and the Democrats sought Owens's support. Although he had always held moderate political views, Owens saw this as an opportunity for income. Many expected him to support Roosevelt, a Democrat. The Democrats were more popular among blacks, and the party

> "When I came back to my native country, after all the stories about Hitler, I couldn't ride in the front of the bus," Owens said. "I had to go to the back door. I couldn't live where I wanted. I wasn't invited to shake hands with Hitler, but I wasn't invited to the White House to shake hands with the president, either."[2]
>
> —*Jesse Owens*

had helped Owens and his family in the past. But Owens decided to support Landon, the Republican candidate. For several weeks, Owens traveled the country speaking to crowds. Much of what he said was not even political, but rather tales of his Olympic experience. To use the famous athlete's name, the Republicans reportedly paid Owens between $10,000 and $15,000. That was a large sum of money, especially when the country was in the midst of the Great Depression. Even with Owens's support, Landon lost in a landslide.

Odd Jobs

For a while, his political work and appearances made Owens quite wealthy. He was able to buy generous gifts for his family and friends. He even bought his parents a new house. But he was not good at managing his money and soon was in need of paying work. The four-time gold medalist also was anxious to return to athletics. Near the end of the year, Owens became the first track athlete and only the second black to be named Associated Press Athlete of the Year. At age 23, he still had a lot of potential. But since he was still banned from amateur athletics by the AAU, he had to find creative ways to compete.

Owens flew to Havana, Cuba, on Christmas Day for the first of what would be many exhibition races. He was not racing against another human. In Cuba, Owens raced against a thoroughbred horse. He beat the horse with a respectable time of 9.9 seconds in the 100-yard dash and earned a hefty $2,000. Some people criticized the Olympic track star for lowering himself to that level. Owens admitted he was embarrassed, but he was also glad to race again while earning a check.

From 1936 to 1939, Owens embarked on a wide array of business ventures. In January 1937, he signed a lucrative contract to tour with a black musical band as their announcer. Upon returning home to Cleveland, he organized a black basketball team called the Olympians. They played for about six months, winning 136 out of 142 games, but did not make very much money.

Meanwhile, Ruth had given birth to their second daughter, Marlene, in 1937.

Great Depression

Beginning in 1929, the United States experienced the Great Depression. This was a period of economic struggles that affected countries all around the world. The United States was affected particularly hard. For the next ten years, unemployment was high and morale was low. In 1936, Owens reportedly earned approximately $26,000. At the time, only 20 percent of people in the United States earned more than $2,000.

Throughout the next four years, Owens worked odd jobs that included a bathhouse supervisor, playground supervisor, and salesman for a local tailor. In August 1938, he joined with two other investors to create The Jesse Owens Dry Cleaning Company. When not working in Cleveland, Owens was often on the road. He continued to travel with the Olympians and with a softball team he created called the Olympics. Life on the road could be challenging. Most restaurants still refused to serve blacks. Racism in general was still

Joe Louis

In June 1937, Joe Louis became the heavyweight boxing champion of the world. He was only the second black man to hold that prestigious title. At a time when white athletes dominated the sports landscape, Louis and Owens were considered among the first black athletes to be universally popular in the United States.

Like Owens, Louis was born in Alabama as the son of a sharecropper and a descendant of slaves. Like Owens, Louis moved north as a child; Louis moved to Detroit, Michigan. As Louis rose to prominence, blacks were often barred from competing for the heavyweight title. He suffered another setback in the weeks before Owens left for the 1936 Olympics. At Yankee Stadium in New York City, Louis lost to German Max Schmeling. The Germans seized that result as an example of Aryan supremacy.

After regaining form and winning the heavyweight title in 1937, "The Brown Bomber" was dominant. He held the title until retiring in 1949 as the longest reigning heavyweight. In 1938, he defeated Schmeling—and in a sense, Nazism—with a first-round knockout. He was highly regarded as a patriotic and unifying man.

rampant. But Owens enjoyed being active on the road. He thrived as an athlete and as a showman.

Back in Cleveland, his partners in the dry cleaning business mismanaged the company. Owens also ran into trouble during the fall of 1938 when he was charged with not paying all of his income taxes. With debt piling up, Owens declared bankruptcy in May 1939. He continued to make exhibition appearances. An all-black baseball team called the Indianapolis Clowns ended each game with Owens racing 60 yards (54.8 m) against a horse. Such stunts affected his reputation, but he felt he was doing what he needed to do to overcome his financial difficulties and support his growing family.

In 1940, Owens began to reevaluate his life. That spring, his mother died, and he was deeply affected by her death. After four years of uncertainty, Owens decided to return to college.

Luz Long

In 1940, Owens received his last letter from Luz Long, his friend from the 1936 Olympics. Long had joined the German army to fight in World War II. In the letter, he asked Owens to find Long's son after the war and to "tell him about the times that war did not separate us— and tell him that things can be different between men in this world."[3] Long died three years later in a British field hospital. He was 30 years old.

Back to School

Owens's third daughter, Beverly, was still a baby when the family moved from Cleveland to Columbus. To pay his tuition, Owens ran a new dry cleaning business and worked with his old coach, Snyder, as an assistant trainer to the college's track team. He wanted to provide for his family.

But once again, Owens struggled. He was so busy with school and working that he did not have much time to spend with his family. In Cleveland, Owens's father died of a heart attack. Even in athletics, Owens had to accept that his feats were fading into the past. The 1940 Olympics had been cancelled due to World War II, but still, some of his records were in danger. At 27 years old, Owens should have been in the prime of his career.

The classroom was still Owens's ultimate challenge. Years before, he had taken mostly easy classes that would not interfere with his training. Now he had to take more advanced classes that would move him closer to graduation. Just as he had with jobs, Owens struggled to focus on school. His grades were poor, but the school made an exception to help him stay enrolled. After four quarters, Owens still could not get his grades up. In December 1941, he dropped out again.

Jesse Owens cleans a shirt at the dry-cleaning business he opened in Cleveland, Ohio, in 1938.

CHAPTER 9

Walter Schreiber, acting mayor of West Berlin, *right*, congratulates Jesse Owens on August 22, 1951.

Stability at Last

After the 1936 Olympics, Germany quickly reinstated its militaristic and discriminatory policies. With Germany's 1939 invasion of Poland, World War II officially started in Europe. The United States did not become involved until 1941 after Japan attacked Pearl Harbor in Hawaii. Within days, the United States was at war with Japan, Germany, and Italy.

In December 1941, shortly after Pearl Harbor was attacked, Owens dropped out of Ohio State. Because he was married and had children, he could not be drafted into the US Army. He soon found another way to represent his country. The federal government hired Owens to travel the country promoting physical fitness programs for blacks. That job led him to Detroit, Michigan, where the family moved in the spring of 1943.

During World War II, the auto manufacturers in Detroit were busy building cars and other machinery for the army. Owens got a job as assistant personnel director with Ford Motor

Company. His job was to work with black employees, helping them to find housing and adjust to their new lives in Detroit. Owens enjoyed his job, and his family was happy in Detroit. But after the company changed ownership, many workers lost their jobs, and Owens was offered a demotion. Rather than accept a lower position, he resigned. A sporting goods store he created failed. So Owens returned to what he knew: traveling the country and cashing in on his name.

Breaking Barriers

During the 1940s, black athletes began to break into the professional sports leagues in the United States that had been limited to whites. In 1942, the National Basketball League allowed ten black players to join two teams. Three years later, in 1945, Kenny Washington and Woody Strode became the first blacks to play in the National Football League in nearly 15 years. In baseball, Jackie Robinson became the first black man to play in the major leagues in more than six decades when he joined the Brooklyn Dodgers in 1946.

The Windy City

In 1949, after nearly four years of travel, Owens decided to move to Chicago, Illinois, where he was offered a job as a promotional executive for a clothing store. Chicago was much larger than Cleveland or Detroit. After struggling to keep a job for so long, he saw an opportunity for more stability in Chicago. He took the job and moved his family there a few months later.

Although Owens found professional success in Chicago, he struggled with his home life. His family was reluctant to leave Detroit. When they finally did, his oldest daughter, Gloria, did not join them. She stayed in Detroit to finish her senior year of high school, where she was class president. Ruth was especially unhappy in Chicago. For years, she had heard rumors that Owens was having affairs. In Chicago, for the first time, she discovered that the rumors were true. She was uncomfortable with the fast-paced life in the big city and heartbroken by her husband's infidelity. But she stayed with Owens. While he worked and traveled, she took on most of the duties of raising Beverly and Marlene.

The Owens's Daughters

After the family left for Chicago, oldest daughter Gloria finished her senior year of high school and then enrolled at Ohio State. In December 1953, she graduated with a degree in education. She was the first member of the family to graduate from college. Their second daughter, Marlene, enrolled at Ohio State in 1956. In 1960, she was the school's homecoming queen, and Owens spoke at the ceremony. The youngest daughter, Beverly, left home to get married in 1956, soon after Marlene moved out.

Owens enjoyed a stable professional life for the first time in Chicago. In 1950, the Associated Press named Owens the best track-and-field athlete from the first half of the century. From 1951 to 1953, he worked with kids as a board member and then executive director of the South Side Boys Club. In 1953, he took a job as the secretary of the Illinois State Athletic Commission. As secretary, Owens supervised the state's amateur and professional boxing matches among other things. The job kept Owens active and in the public eye. He also held positions at various other companies, ran his own public relations company, and continued making appearances and working with kids. He also developed a passion for golf. As one of his secretaries said, "He's the busiest man I ever saw."[1]

Owens enjoyed being in a position of respect. He was finally beginning to be recognized in the way he expected to be back in 1936. Now, the public began to recognize Owens's second great strength—his speaking

Revisiting Berlin

In 1951, Owens returned to Berlin for the first time since the 1936 Olympics. Hitler and Nazi Germany had been defeated in World War II approximately six years earlier. Now the country and the city of Berlin were split in two: East and West. When Owens returned to the friendly West Germany in 1951, he was again greeted as a hero.

A crowd of 75,000 people waited at the Olympic Stadium, where Owens had won four gold medals 15 years before. This time, Owens was in Germany with the Harlem Globetrotters, a basketball team. But before the game, the 37-year-old Owens spoke to the crowd. Afterward, the mayor of West Berlin approached the microphone. "Hitler wouldn't shake your hand," he said to Owens. "I give you both hands."[2] The crowd roared as the mayor shook Owens's hands in both of his.

Following the game, Owens met Luz Long's son, Kai. Owens would later return to Berlin in 1966 to film a documentary called *Jesse Owens Returns to Berlin*, along with filmmaker Bud Greenspan.

ability. His popularity grew because of his moderate viewpoints, open demeanor, and success as a black man. He traveled the country telling his rags-to-riches story and talking about what it was like to embarrass Hitler in Berlin. He spoke about the great opportunities America offered. He especially enjoyed working with children. Owens wanted to help them achieve their dreams as he had done. Owens's reputation and popularity continued to grow. Soon, President Dwight Eisenhower called on him to act as a goodwill ambassador. Owens traveled to India, Malaya, and the Philippines in the fall of 1955. The next summer, White House officials asked Owens to represent the president at the 1956 Olympics in Melbourne, Australia. Eisenhower continued to use Owens in similar roles.

In November 1955, Owens took a new job as executive director of the Illinois Youth Commission. In this job, he traveled around the state promoting different programs to help keep kids out of trouble. Additional income from the speaking circuit kept Owens and his family financially comfortable.

"He remains one of the most magnetic of all sports heroes. People who have never met him idolize him. He has accepted this as part of his life, and he does not want to rock the boat. . . . Now, 28 years after his Olympic glory, Jesse Owens is a happy man. He is successful in business, he is a renowned speaker, he is a grandfather four times, and he is a man at peace with himself."[3]
—*New York Times, 1964*

Ups and Downs

In 1960, Owens cofounded the public relations firm Owens-West & Associates. While his partner, Ted West, managed the business, Owens spent most of his time elsewhere. He was often on the road giving speeches or doing promotional work for other companies. Many companies, such as Quaker Oats and Meister Brausing Beer Company, were now paying Owens to promote their products. But in 1961, his political career hit a bump. A Republican governor had appointed Owens to his position with the Illinois Youth Commission. After a Democrat took office, Owens lost his job for supporting a controversial union leader.

Into the 1960s, Owens received more business and speaking offers than he could possibly accept. After working as an exercise coach at the New York Mets spring-training workouts in 1965, he hit another obstacle. First, a ruptured disc in his spine required surgery. As he was recovering, the Internal Revenue Service took him to trial for failing to pay income taxes from 1959 to 1962. Owens faced a potential $40,000 fine and four-year jail sentence. Owens had never been good at managing his finances. He knew he had not paid the taxes. On February 1, the judge made Owens pay $68,166 in back taxes and a small fine without a jail sentence, citing the athlete's strong record of public service.

In 1964, Jesse Owens visits the Olympic stadium in Berlin where he won four gold medals in 1936.

CHAPTER 10

President Gerald Ford poses with Jesse Owens after Owens is honored with the Presidential Medal of Freedom.

A Legend

The United States experienced political changes during the 1960s. After years of suffering discrimination, some blacks were beginning to take a more aggressive approach toward gaining equality. This was called the Black Power movement, and those involved were often outspoken. The nation was engaged in an unpopular war in Vietnam. Many people began staging protests and demonstrations.

Owens, now in his fifties, was disappointed and confused by the actions of the younger people. He had always held conservative viewpoints and an intense patriotism. He believed that patience and working together with whites would correct the injustices. "I started from the bottom—and look at me now," he once said. "I've got two homes, and I'm free to travel, and I know where my next meals are coming from."[1] But many within the Black Power community despised Owens. They accused him of being naïve and brainwashed by whites.

Tommie Smith and John Carlos salute the Black Power movement during their medal ceremony at the 1968 Olympics.

An Olympic Protest

The 1968 Olympics took place in Mexico City, Mexico. Owens was invited to attend as a guest of the Mexican government. He also worked as a radio commentator and as a liaison between the US Olympic

Committee (USOC) and the US black athletes.
Before the Olympics, some US blacks had considered
boycotting the games. They did not want to represent
the United States when the laws of the country treated
them as second-class citizens. Their boycott would
weaken the US team and also embarrass the Olympic
movement, which was supposed to be apolitical. As
in 1936, Owens opposed a boycott. He considered the
Olympics to be a rare opportunity and athletes could
use it as a springboard to other successes. Eventually,
most of the top US athletes decided to participate.
But the USOC was still worried that some might try to
make a political statement during the games.

On the fourth day of competition, Tommie Smith,
a black US sprinter, won the 200-meter dash. His
black teammate John Carlos finished third. Both were
proponents of the Black Power movement, and both
had strongly considered boycotting. Instead, they made
their protest on the medal stand. Neither wore shoes
on the podium; instead they wore black socks. As the
national anthem played, the two men lowered their
heads—against Olympic protocol—and each raised one
arm. With black gloves on one hand, each clenched his
fist—the symbol of Black Power.

Pictures of Smith and Carlos on the podium
became symbolic for the civil rights movement. Many
looked at the two athletes as being brave for standing

up for what they believed. Others, however, did not. Olympic officials, and Owens, were embarrassed. After the incident, the International Olympic Committee suspended the athletes. The USOC immediately sent Owens to talk to Smith and Carlos in an attempt to convince them to apologize. Owens found that he was unable to connect with the younger generation. Black and white athletes alike came to the protestors' support, and neither athlete ended up apologizing.

Black Power

During the 1960s, some blacks began taking a more aggressive approach toward acquiring civil rights in the United States. This was called the Black Power movement. Before that, most blacks believed that working together with open-minded whites was the best way to gain equality. The Black Power advocates believed blacks should rely only on themselves to improve their social, economic, and political standing.

The movement was credited with improving awareness of black culture and instilling feelings of pride and freedom among blacks. Black Power also had its critics—black and white. They blamed the movement for using violence and militant tactics to draw attention to their cause. Others believed that the movement was creating a bigger divide between black and white cultures.

The Black Power movement ended in the early 1970s. Black Power had been an offshoot of the civil rights movement of the 1950s and 1960s.

Owens supported the more conservative, nonviolent views on civil rights held by blacks such as Martin Luther King Jr. These views ultimately proved to be more popular and unifying.

Political Authoring

Upon returning home, Owens wanted to show that all blacks did not share the same beliefs as Jones and Carlos. Along with ghostwriter Paul Neimark, Owens wrote a book called *Blackthink*. In it, he denounced black militancy and said that blacks needed to work harder within the current system. "If the Negro doesn't succeed in today's America," he wrote, "it is because he has chosen to fail. Yes, there are exceptions. But there are exceptions for whites, too."[2] The book was well received among whites. But many blacks disagreed with Owens's views.

Facing criticism, Owens had second thoughts about what he had written. Two years later, in 1972, Owens wrote *I Have Changed* with Neimark. In it, Owens apologized for much of what he wrote in his first book and explained what made him write it. In regards to his comment about failing, Owens wrote:

> *Deep down, I knew better. There aren't near as many exceptions if your skin is white. But I'd wanted so badly to tell the young blacks they did have a chance, if only they'd work twice as hard and turn the other cheek when the first one was maybe raw and open to the bone. I'd wanted to tell them too badly.*[3]

The Last Record

In 1975, the last of Owens's world records finally fell. Forty years after Owens set the mark, Cliff Outlin beat the record time in the indoor 60-meter dash by 0.2 seconds. "Sure, I'm a little sad," Owens said afterward. "It's like losing a member of the family."[4]

Jesse Owens, 60, chats with fans before the Big Ten Outdoor Track Championships in 1974.

Always on the Move

Even in old age, Owens constantly needed to be active. In the early 1970s, he was traveling more than 200,000 miles (322,000 km) each year giving 80 to 90 speeches and making other promotional appearances for various companies. Owens spent an average of four nights each week in a hotel room. He and Ruth lived comfortably with Owens earning approximately $75,000 yearly. Despite their earlier problems, Owens and Ruth worked out their issues and stayed together. In the early 1970s, they left Chicago for Scottsdale, Arizona, which was warmer and had less commotion. In 1974, Owens was inducted into the USA Track and Field Hall of Fame in New York City. Two years later, President Gerald Ford awarded Owens the Medal of Freedom, the highest civilian honor.

Owens continued his busy speaking and promotional schedule until he no longer could. In the late autumn of 1979, he began feeling weak

Back in Berlin

In 2009, the US track-and-field team returned to Berlin for the first time since 1936 for the World Track and Field Champi-onships. "The first thing I thought of was how intimidating and impos-ing it was, just the rocks with all the columns," Stephanie Brown Trafton, a discus thrower, said of the Olympic Stadium. "I imagined how Jesse felt walking into the sta-dium in a situation where people definitely weren't rooting for him."[5] The US athletes wore a patch with Owens's initials above their hearts while they competed. "The 'JO' on the uniform lets me know it's bigger than just me running for myself," sprinter LaShawn Merritt said. "It's for my country and the history."[6]

> "If I had to do it all over again, I probably would. More people have been kind to me than not, and they have looked upon my accomplishments more than the color of my skin. I have led a happy life, and I am a happy man."[8]
> —*Jesse Owens*

and sick. By December, he was no longer able to work. Upon checking into a hospital, Owens found out that he had lung cancer. Out of the public's sight, Owens had been a smoker for almost 30 years. The doctors gave him three months to live. On March 31, 1980, Owens died at a hospital in Tucson, Arizona. He was 66.

In Alabama and Ohio, monuments were built in his honor. Ohio State named its track and a nearby plaza after him. In Berlin, a road by the Olympic stadium was named in his honor. Owens is remembered for his incredible feats on the track. But in his later years, he also became known for his inspirational speaking abilities and for his commitment to helping young people. And it was for those qualities that Owens most wanted to be recognized. "Awards become tarnished, and diplomas fade. . . . Championships are mythical things. They have no permanence," Owens once remarked. He went on to wonder if people who heard him speak went on to tell their loved ones his message. "Then I think, that's immortality. You are immortal if your ideas are being passed on from a father to his son and to his son and to his son, and on and on."[7]

A statue of Jesse Owens at the Jesse Owens Memorial Park in Oakville, Alabama

1913

James Cleveland Owens is born in Oakville, Alabama, on September 12.

1922

The Owens family moves to Cleveland, Ohio.

1927

Owens begins training for track and field with Charles Riley.

1932

Ruth Solomon gives birth to Gloria Shirley Owens on August 8.

1933

Owens sets a world record in the 220-yard dash and ties the world record in the 100-yard dash at the National Interscholastic Championship.

1933

Owens enrolls at Ohio State University.

1928

Owens sets junior high school world records in long jump and high jump.

1930

Owens enrolls at East Technical High School in Cleveland.

1932

Owens does not qualify for the Summer Olympics in Los Angeles, California.

1935

At the Big Ten Conference meet, Owens sets three world records and ties another.

1935

Owens marries Ruth Solomon on July 5.

1935

The AAU investigates whether Owens was being overpaid for his job as a page.

1935

Despite strong opposition, the AAU votes against boycotting the 1936 Olympics.

1936

In July, Owens is one of 18 black athletes to qualify for the 1936 Olympics.

1936

Owens wins four gold medals at the 1936 Olympics in Berlin, Germany.

1943

The Owens family moves to Detroit, Michigan, where Owens works for Ford Motor Company.

1968

The Owens family moves to Chicago, Illinois. Owens continues traveling and working in other jobs.

1968

At the 1968 Olympics, two black athletes raise their fists to protest for black rights on the medal stand.

1936	**1936**	**1940**
Owens leaves a tour of Europe to pursue opportunities at home.	In an exhibition race in December, Jesse Owens races a horse.	Jesse, Ruth, and their three daughters move to Columbus, Ohio, and Owens reenrolls in Ohio State.

1970	**1976**	**1980**
Owens writes *Blackthink*.	Owens receives the Medal of Freedom.	Owens dies of lung cancer in Arizona in March.

ESSENTIAL FACTS

DATE OF BIRTH
September 12, 1913

PLACE OF BIRTH
Oakville, Alabama

DATE OF DEATH
March 31, 1980

PLACE OF DEATH
Tucson, Arizona

PARENTS
Henry Cleveland Owens and Emma Fitzgerald

EDUCATION
Ohio State University (never graduated)

MARRIAGE
Ruth Solomon, July 5, 1935

CHILDREN
Gloria, Marlene, and Beverly

CAREER HIGHLIGHTS

As a senior at East Tech High School, Owens set a world record in the 220-yard dash and tied the world record in the 100-yard dash. At the 1935 Big Ten Conference meet, Owens tied his world record in the 100-yard dash, and set world records in the broad jump, 220-yard dash, and 220-yard hurdles. At the 1936 Olympics, Owens won four gold medals while German chancellor Adolf Hitler looked on.

SOCIAL CONTRIBUTIONS

At the 1936 Olympics, Owens inspired people around the world by winning four gold medals. He achieved this despite being discriminated against because of his skin color. Later in life, President Gerald Ford presented Owens with the Medal of Freedom for his work as an inspirational speaker and positive example for young people. He also spent time in the latter part of his life promoting more conservative methods of achieving racial equality in the United States.

CONFLICTS

Owens grew up and spent much of his life in a country with legalized segregation. Before the 1936 Olympics in Berlin, Germany, Owens was pressured to boycott but chose not to. Upon quitting an exhibition circuit following the Olympics, he was banned from amateur athletics. When he returned to the United States, Owens struggled to find a stable job. Later in life, Owens disagreed with members of the Black Power movement over how to achieve civil rights.

QUOTE

"In America, anyone can become somebody. Does that sound corny in this day and age? Well, it happened to me, and I believe it can happen to anybody in one way or another."
—*Jesse Owens*

GLOSSARY

ambassador
A person serving as an official representative for something.

apolitical
Having no interest in politics.

bankrupt
Unable to pay off debts.

bogus
Not genuine.

bootlegging
The making, moving, and selling of alcohol, which was illegal in the 1920s.

deacon
An assistant to a priest or minister.

democracy
A government in which every person has the right to participate, often by electing representatives.

dictatorship
When one person has absolute power over a government.

discrimination
Unfair treatment of a person or group based on a particular trait, such as race or religion.

endorsement
The public support of a product or company.

fibrous tumor
A noncancerous lump on the body.

ghostwriter
An author who helps write a book but is not credited.

integrated
    When members of different races are not separated, such as
    at a school.

lynch
    To put somebody to death without trial, often by hanging.

page
    A young person who acts as a servant or assistant to a
    member of a legislative body.

propaganda
    Information put out by a government to sway public opinion
    in support of its policies.

proponent
    A person who argues in favor of something.

segregation
    The separation of people based on racial, religious, or other
    traits.

vocational school
    A secondary school that trains its students for a specific
    trade or skill to be used in a career.

ADDITIONAL RESOURCES

SELECTED BIBLIOGRAPHY

Baker, William J. *Jesse Owens: An American Life*. New York: Free Press, 1986.

Owens, Jesse, with Paul Neimark. *Jesse, a Spiritual Autobiography*. Plainfield, NJ: Logos International, 1978.

Schaap, Jeremy. *Triumph: The Untold Story of Jesse Owens and Hitler's Olympics*. Boston, MA: Houghton Mifflin, 2007.

Snyder, Larry. "My Boy Jesse." *The Saturday Evening Post*. 7 Nov. 1936. 14–15, 97–101.

FURTHER READINGS

Edmondson, Jacqueline. *Jesse Owens: A Biography*. Westport, CT: Greenwood Press, 2007.

Gifford, Clive. *Summer Olympics: The Definitive Guide to the World's Greatest Sports Celebration*. Boston, MA: Kingfisher, 2004.

Hilton, Christopher. *Hitler's Olympics: The 1936 Berlin Olympic Games*. Charleston, SC: The History Press, 2008.

Israel, Elaine. *Jesse Owens: Running Into History*. New York: Collins, 2008.

Owens, Jesse. *Track and Field*. New York: Atheneum, 1976.

WEB LINKS

To learn more about Jesse Owens, visit ABDO Publishing Company online at **www.abdopublishing.com**. Web sites about Jesse Owens are featured on our Book Links page. These links are routinely monitored and updated to provide the most current information available.

PLACES TO VISIT

Jesse Owens Memorial Park Museum
7019 County Road 203, Danville, AL 35619
256-974-3636
www.jesseowensmuseum.org
The museum features memorabilia and replicas from Owens's life. In *Return to Berlin*, Owens narrates a film about the 1936 Olympics. The museum is located in a park, which also features tributes to Owens. Admission to the museum is free for groups less than ten.

National Track & Field Hall of Fame
216 Fort Washington Avenue, Washington Heights, NY 10032
http://www.usatf.org/HallOfFame/TF/
Visitors can learn about track and field and what it takes to be an athlete through videos and interactive exhibits. A Walk of Fame features the names of the hall of fame members. The facility is also home to an indoor track-and-field arena.

Olympiastadion Berlin (Olympic Stadium)
Olympischer Platz 3
14053 Berlin, Germany
Telephone: +49-030–306 88 100
http://www.olympiastadion-berlin.de/index.php?id=1&L=1
The 1936 Olympic Stadium provides guided tours that include otherwise private areas while documenting the stadium's history, architecture, and technology. Tours are in German.

SOURCE NOTES

CHAPTER 1. An Unlikely Friend

1. Jeremy Schaap. "The Olympian and the Dictator." *Runner's World*. March 2007. Print. 117, 121.

2. Jeremy Schaap. *Triumph: The Untold Story of Jesse Owens and Hitler's Olympics*. Boston, MA: Houghton Mifflin, 2007. Print. 209.

3. William J. Baker. *Jesse Owens: An American Life*. New York: Free Press, 1986. Print. 237.

4. Larry Schwartz. "Owens pierced a myth." *ESPN.com*. Web. 6 July 2010.

CHAPTER 2. Son of a Sharecropper

1. William J. Baker. *Jesse Owens: An American Life*. New York: Free Press, 1986. Print. 9–10.

2. Jeremy Schaap. *Triumph: The Untold Story of Jesse Owens and Hitler's Olympics*. Boston, MA: Houghton Mifflin, 2007. Print. 20.

3. William J. Baker. *Jesse Owens: An American Life*. New York: Free Press, 1986. Print. 11.

4. Ibid. 16.

CHAPTER 3. Moving to Ohio

1. Jeremy Schaap. *Triumph: The Untold Story of Jesse Owens and Hitler's Olympics*. Boston, MA: Houghton Mifflin, 2007. Print. 21.

2. William J. Baker. *Jesse Owens: An American Life*. New York: Free Press, 1986. Print. 25.

3. Jeremy Schaap. *Triumph: The Untold Story of Jesse Owens and Hitler's Olympics*. Boston, MA: Houghton Mifflin, 2007. Print. 24.

CHAPTER 4. The Buckeye Bullet

1. William J. Baker. *Jesse Owens: An American Life*. New York: Free Press, 1986. Print. 35.

2. Ibid.

3. Ibid. 45.

4. Jeremy Schaap. *Triumph: The Untold Story of Jesse Owens and Hitler's Olympics*. Boston, MA: Houghton Mifflin, 2007. Print. 11.

CHAPTER 5. A Series of Setbacks

1. William J. Baker. *Jesse Owens: An American Life*. New York: Free Press, 1986. Print. 56–57.

2. Jeremy Schaap. "The Olympian and the Dictator." *Runner's World*. March 2007. Print. 79.

3. "Sport: Games at Garmisch." *TIME*. 17 Feb. 1936. Web. 6 July 2010.

4. Jeremy Schaap. *Triumph: The Untold Story of Jesse Owens and Hitler's Olympics*. Boston, MA: Houghton Mifflin, 2007. Print. 98.

CHAPTER 6. The 1936 Olympics

1. Jeremy Schaap. *Triumph: The Untold Story of Jesse Owens and Hitler's Olympics*. Boston, MA: Houghton Mifflin, 2007. Print. 170.

2. Arthur J. Daley. "Owens Captures Olympic Title, Equals World 100-Meter Record." *New York Times*. 4 Aug. 1936. Print. 1.

3. William J. Baker. *Jesse Owens: An American Life*. New York: Free Press, 1986. Print. 91.

4. Larry Snyder. "My Boy Jesse." *The Saturday Evening Post*. 7 Nov. 1936. Print. 97.

5. Jeremy Schaap. *Triumph: The Untold Story of Jesse Owens and Hitler's Olympics*. Boston, MA: Houghton Mifflin, 2007. Print. 191.

CHAPTER 7. No Longer an Amateur

1. Associated Press. "Owens to Turn Pro If Offers Suit Him."
New York Times. 11 Aug. 1936. Print. 26.

2. William J. Baker. *Jesse Owens: An American Life.* New
York: Free Press, 1986. Print. 120.

3. Ibid.

4. Associated Press. "Caustic Comment by Snyder." *New
York Times.* 17 Aug. 1936. Print. 11.

5. Associated Press. "Owens to Turn Pro If Offers Suit Him."
New York Times. 11 Aug. 1936. Print. 26.

6. Larry Snyder. "My Boy Jesse." *The Saturday Evening
Post.* 7 Nov. 1936. Print. 98.

7. Jesse Owens with Paul Neimark. *Jesse, a Spiritual
Autobiography.* Plainfield, NJ: Logos International, 1978.
Print. 81.

CHAPTER 8. Money Maker

1. "National Affairs: Owens for Landon." *TIME.* 14 Sept.
1936. Web. 6 July 2010.

2. Larry Schwartz. "Owens pierced a myth." *ESPN.com.*
Web. 6 July 2010.

3. Jeremy Schaap. *Triumph: The Untold Story of Jesse
Owens and Hitler's Olympics.* Boston, MA: Houghton Mifflin,
2007. Print. 235.

CHAPTER 9. Stability at Last

1. William J. Baker. *Jesse Owens: An American Life.* New
York: Free Press, 1986. Print. 176.

2. "75,000 In Berlin Hail Jesse Owens." *New York Times.* 23
Aug. 1951. Print. 37.

3. "Owens Still Sets a Swift Pace." *New York Times.* 22 Nov.
1964. Print. S8.

CHAPTER 10. A Legend

1. William J. Baker. *Jesse Owens: An American Life*. New York: Free Press, 1986. Print. 205.

2. Jesse Owens, with Paul G. Neimark. *Blackthink: My Life as Black Man and White Man*. New York: Morrow, 1970. Print. 44.

3. Jesse Owens, with Paul Neimark. *I Have Changed*. New York: Morrow, 1972. Print. 9–10.

4. Associated Press. "Jesse unforgettable: Last Owens record broken." *The (Bend) Bulletin*. 5 Feb. 1975. 15. Web. 6 July 2010.

5. Philip Hersh. "Jesse Owens' exploits still echo at Berlin's Olympic Stadium." *Los Angeles Times*. 15 Aug. 2009. Web. 6 July 2010.

6. Ibid.

7. William Johnson. "After The Golden Moment." *Sports Illustrated*. 17 July 1972. Web. 6 July 2010.

8. "Owens Still Sets a Swift Pace." *New York Times*. 22 Nov. 1964. Print. S8.

INDEX

ABOUT THE AUTHOR

Chrös McDougall is a sports writer and editor. As a sports reporter, he has covered a variety of events, from the Beijing Olympics to college football, basketball, and gymnastics. He currently works as an editor. He lives in the Twin Cities with his wife, Jill.

PHOTO CREDITS

LEGENDARY ATHLETES